INHALE DEEP!

A 3 day girl's guide to loving herself 1st

Published by
ButterflyBlue Publishing Co.

2019

ISBN: 978-0-578-48111-1 (paperback)

Inhale Deep: A 3-day girl's guide to loving herself 1st.

Printed in the United States of America.

Contributions by Nikiea Redmond, Saché Jones, and the cast of the *Anatomy of Wings* Documentary.

Illustrations by Christina Brown, Nikiea & Envato Elements.

Book Design by Nikiea.

Edited by Mia Loving, InvisibleMajority & Sarah Wallace, Vision to Life.

BECOME A SPONSOR OR ORDER BULK COPIES
AT BUTTERFLYBLUEBOOKS@GMAIL.COM

iINSTAGRAM: @BUTTERFLYBLUEBOOKS

Dedicated to Jordyn,
Caché, Morgan, Raven, Learra
and every girl finding her wings.

SELF
LOVE
CLUB

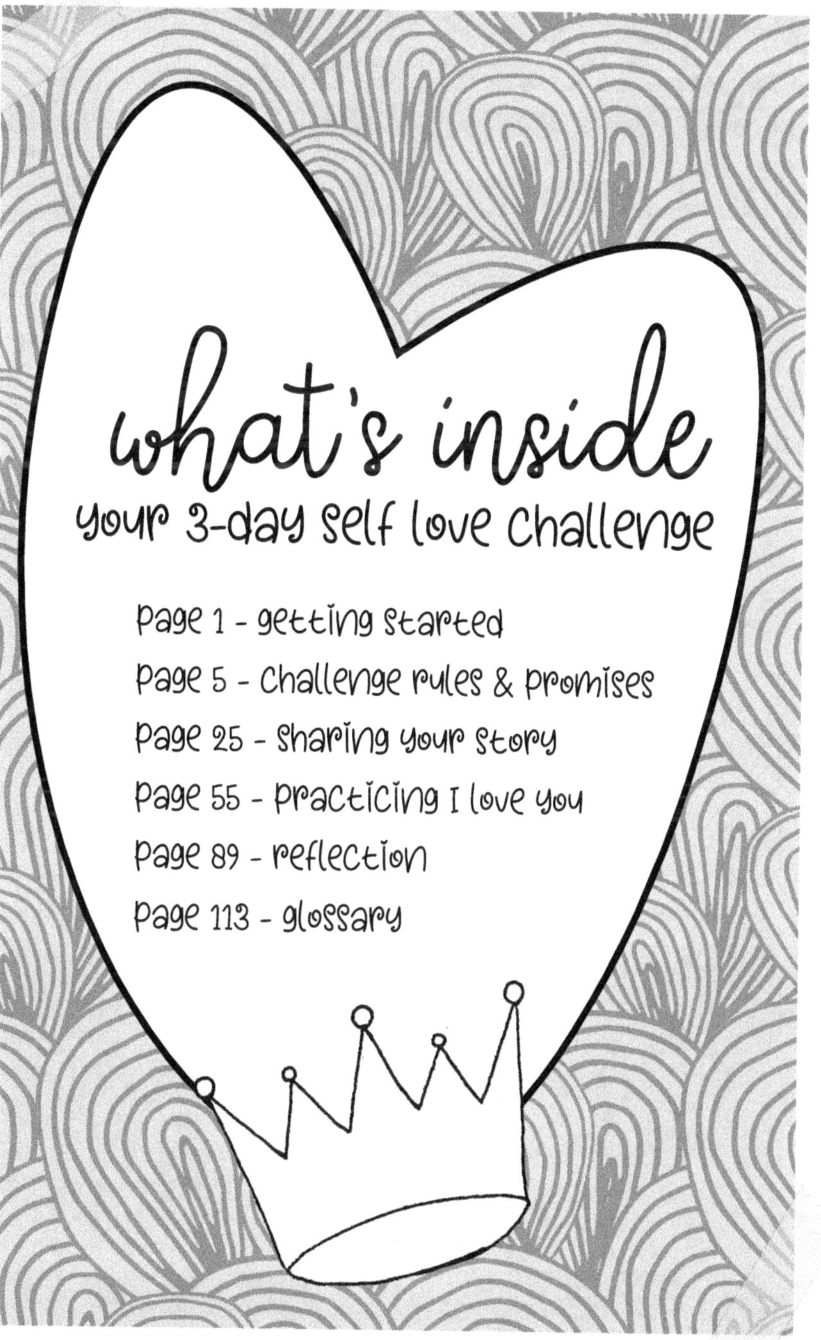

page 1 - getting started

page 5 - challenge rules & promises

page 25 - sharing your story

page 55 - practicing I love you

page 89 - reflection

page 113 - glossary

you are
worth so much.

You might be the girl that loves sparkles or maybe you're the girl that loves shooting free throws on the basketball court. No matter who you are, you can find examples of love all around you. Love is universal. This 3 day self love challenge is for every girl creating space & time to practice loving herself!

Let's Get Started!

Love is a feeling. Love is an action. Love is safe. Love is ________________________________.

Whether you love to sing or love to draw or love to eat cupcakes; you have practiced saying "love", feeling love, and sharing love. Over the next three days, challenge yourself to choose loving you first. Explore what you need to feel loved in every way. This guide is your creative space. Write, draw, or color to share your experience as you practice this beautiful act of loving yourself.

Girl, you Got This!

#baltimorehugstoo #justbreathe #girlsselflovejournal

controlling your breath

breathe

Deep breathing is an activity I do for myself when I feel frustrated, angry, or anxious. I **close my eyes** or softly stare at a wall or object. I **Inhale deeply** with my hand over My stomach, **filling my body with air**. I Hold my breath for a second. Then **exhale blowing all the air out** through my nose, listening to the sound of my breath. With each breath I focus on my breath to relax my thoughts and detach myself from distractions.

⚡ Try deep breathing ten times today. Inhale Deep & Exhale.

how to start

rules
- and -
promises

repeat this 3 times to yourself
in your mind or aloud.

take a break & try

a 30 minute walk in a park around grass, trees and fresh air
with friend or guardian
hugging a tree
saying positive words in the mirror
saying positive words with I AM in the mirror
sharing a story of love
watching the clouds
praying
meditating
drinking a few glasses of water
try ginger tea, peppermint tea, chamomile tea
break from Instagram and Facebook
riding a bike
drawing
painting
writing
watch waves at the beach
massage your own ankles, hands, neck or feet
learning a yoga pose
making a private video diary
volunteering with a community project
reading a motivational book
watching motivational videos on YouTube

The world is following your example of
how to treat you.

creating safe space

Let's imagine

Close your eyes and think of
the safest space you can create
for yourself.

What does this space smell like?
What does your space feel like?
What sounds do you hear?

Open your eyes and draw or describe your safe space. Use crayons, markers or colored pencils to highlight the favorite parts of your space.

FREE SPACE: DRAW OR WRITE

FREE SPACE: DRAW OR WRITE

trust your gut
IT'S OKAY TO SAY NO TO TAKE CARE OF YOU.

No.

Nope.

I would appreciate if you listened to me, I said no.

No, That doesn't make me feel comfortable.

No, I'm not interested.

Not right now, thank you though.

Not today.

Sometimes saying no
means saying yes to yourself.
**What ways can you respectfully
say no to feel safe?**

yoga & exercise

Practice being grateful for your body! **Respecting your body's boundaries** and nourishing your body with **exercise, water, sunlight, rest, vegetables** and patience.

Try the
Tree Pose

Stand Tall. Like a Tree.

Shoulders relaxed.

Lift your right leg,
bending your right knee
towards your thigh or
as high as you can.

Hold this position &
countdown from 10 to 1.

**If your leg falls, it's okay,
try again until you're comfortable
holding the Tree Pose
for 10 seconds.**

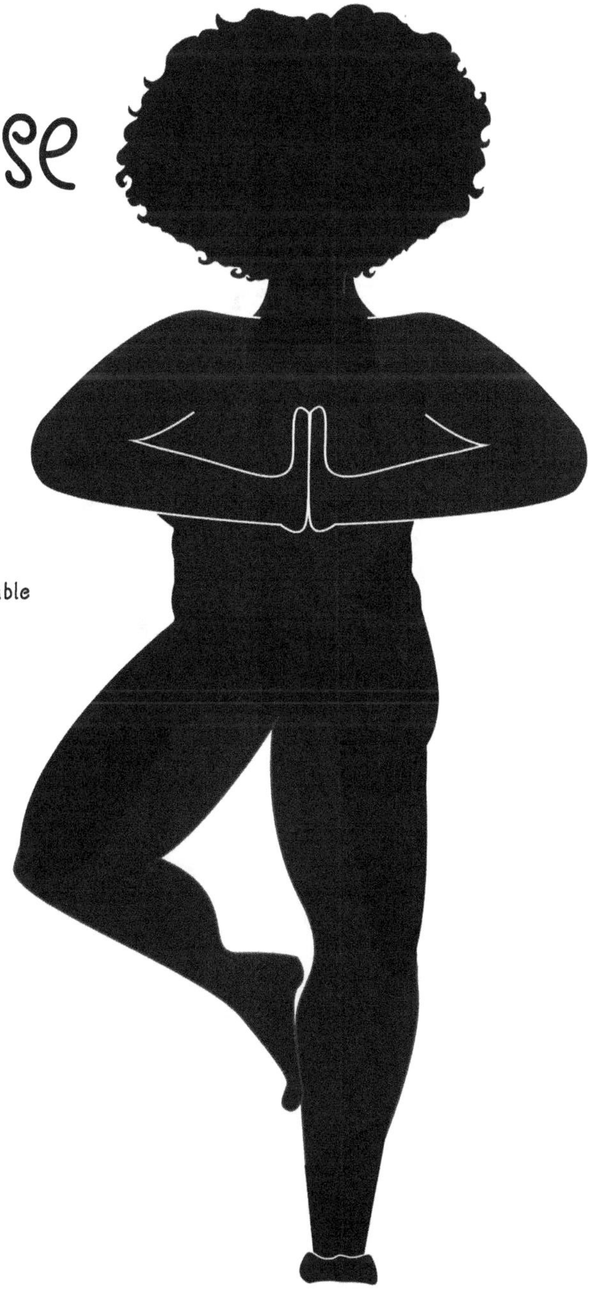

Eating
to Nourish
your Body

things to eat

Fresh Vegetables

kale greens, collard greens, carrots, spinach

Fresh Fruit:

strawberry, banana, pineapple, starfruit, blueberry, mango

things to drink

7 cups of water each day

Organic Tea: peppermint tea, chamomile tea, ginger tea

How to make ginger tea (with a guardian)

ingredients

one ginger root *the size of the palm of your hand*
water
a small pot

cooking instructions

- Take the ginger root and gently wash it.
- Use your hands to break the ginger root in three or four pieces.
- Grab your small pot (with an adult) add the ginger root & add water almost to the top.
- Place small pot on the stove.
- Ask your guardian to turn the stove on medium high.
- As the water starts to boil you'll start smelling the ginger cooking.
- Turn the stove down to low-medium heat.
- Let the ginger boil for another 10 minutes.
- Turn the small pot off.

Let the ginger tea sit/steep for 15 minutes.
Pour a glass, add honey or a little sugar and enjoy!

Make a list of healthy recipes or create your own.

How to make delicious diffused water with fruit and veggies.

ingredients

lemon, lime, basil leaf

clear water bottle, 8oz or larger

making diffused water

- Wash the lemon, lime and one basil leaf.
- Use your hands to rip the lemon in four chunks. Then rip the lime in four chunks.
- Fill your water bottle with warm water.
- Add two lemon chunks and two lime chunks with the basil leaf to your water bottle.
- Add the top securely on your water bottle and shake two times.

Drink & enjoy or

Let the water sit for 15 minutes on the counter.

You can also use cucumber, berries, and pineapple

and other fruits to diffuse your water.

[ASK YOUR GUARDIAN IF YOU HAVE FOOD ALLERGIES BEFORE TRYING THESE RECIPES.]

smells that
energize

Lemon & Citrus fruits

Squeeze a lemon, Peel it and Smell the lemon peel.
Lemons have a natural scent that energizes your mind.

Essential oils are natural oils from plants that

are used to create smells that give your body, mind
and emotions a boost of energy. These oils should be
used carefully they are fine to touch but sometimes not
okay to eat, drink, or get close to your eyes.

Each oil smells different some are strong scents and
some are soft scents. Find an oil that you love and try
placing three drops on your favorite pillow or rubbed
on back of your hand.

Lavender, Lemongrass, Rosemary, Peppermint are a
few great oils to try with a guardian.

smells to pay attention to on your 3-day self love challenge.

smoke smells
musty smells
rotten smells

If you have these smells in your safe space or at home. Keep lemon peel with you in a ziplock bag or napkin. Break a piece and smell it to give your senses a break. You can also open a window or clean your area with a clean cloth, water and a drop of soap or sweep the floor and take out the trash.

Smells are important for your focus.
Use natural scents to help you.

List 5 smells you love. Why do you love them?

day one
1
Tell Your Story

share

morning routine

Create your safe space

Close your eyes.
Inhale Deep
Exhale
(repeat 5 times)
Open your eyes.

List 5 things you are grateful for this morning.

List 5 things you love about yourself.

FREE SPACE: DRAW OR WRITE

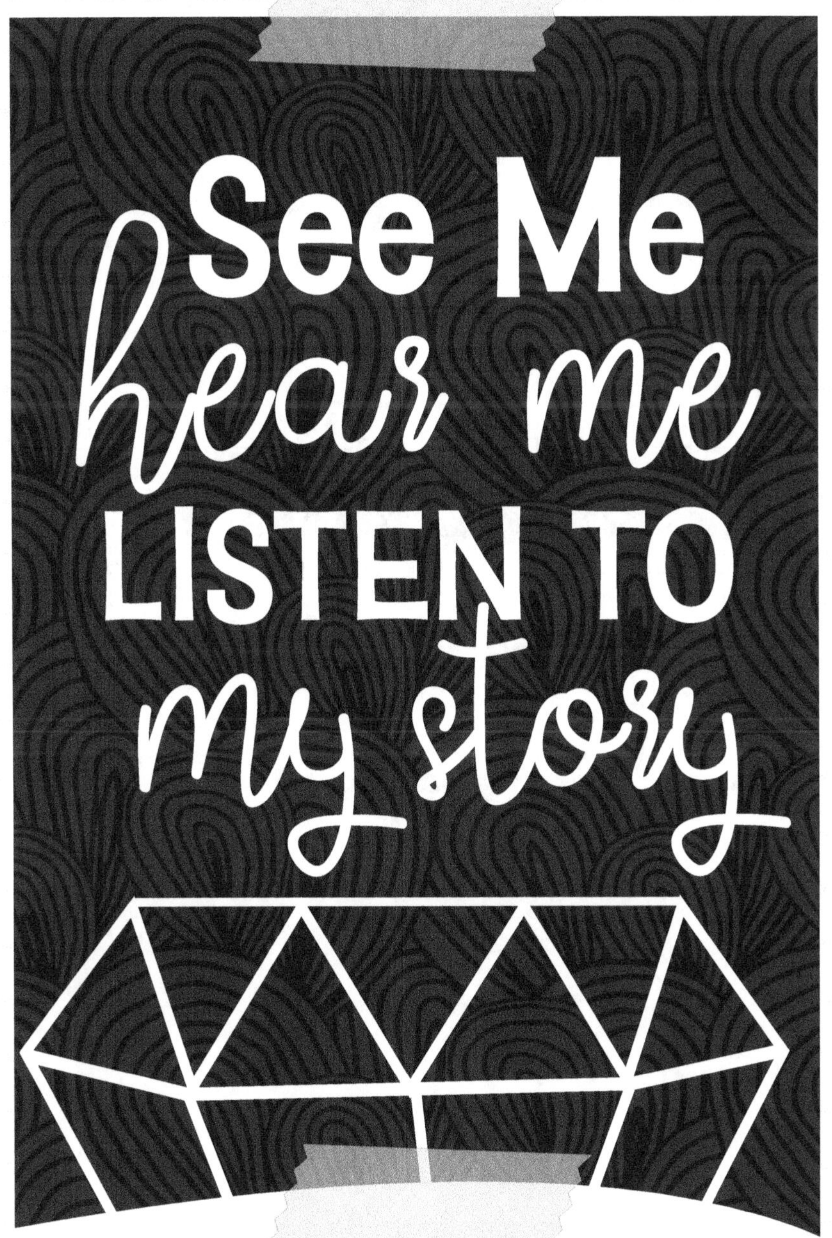
See Me
hear me
LISTEN TO
my story

use the next pages to write your story.

Who are you?

Who do you think you are?

What kind of feelings are you holding on to today?

What makes you feel?

How do you see love?

Who are you?

Who do you think you are?

What kind of feelings are you holding on to today?

What makes you feel?

How do you see love?

list 5 ways you can
shower yourself
with love

FREE SPACE: DRAW OR WRITE

I love
ME today,
tomorrow,
and forever.

FREE SPACE: DRAW OR WRITE

FREE SPACE: DRAW OR WRITE

What does love mean to you?

Love starts from within. In order to find love you must first find yourself and love your flaws and all.

FREE SPACE: DRAW OR WRITE

FREE SPACE: DRAW OR WRITE

what makes
you feel and
look beautiful?

Draw your
favorite
outfit.

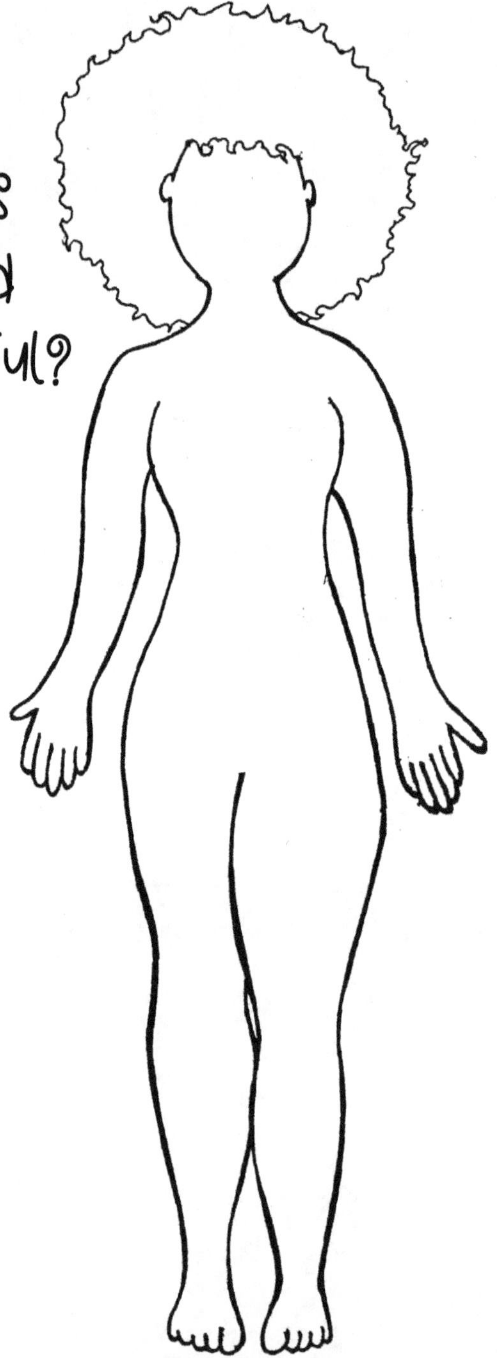

Beautiful Girl,
you can do
AMAZING
things.

FREE SPACE: DRAW OR WRITE

What makes you feel safe?

Draw a space you feel safe in

Draw a space you feel safe in

tonight's reflection

What was it like to love yourself 1st today?

List 10 things you are grateful for.

day two
learning how to say I love you
2

practice

morning routine

Create your safe space

Close your eyes.
Inhale Deep
Exhale
(repeat 5 times)
Open your eyes.

List 5 things you are grateful for this morning.

List 5 things you love about yourself.

FREE SPACE: DRAW OR WRITE

```
E X C E L L E N T I U A O P E A C E F U L C B N F S T R O N G
G Q L P D E T E R M I N E D Y U O S C O M P A S S I O N A T E
C R E A T I V E W C G B K I N D W T U A S S E R T I V E I S H D I L I G E N T
T H A N K F U L F A S C F R I E N D L Y N W R T H A P P Y
I N T E L L I G E N T B Q X T R U S T W O R T H Y B D J R E S P E C T F U L
D E T A C H E D M H M C O N F I D E N T P T Y U A C C E P T I N G E D H C I N S P I R E D
L O V I N G F T J H O N O R A B L E O T G O A L - D R I V E N B H C A R I N G U E D S
A B L E M L C O M F O R T A B L E E D T A M A Z I N G G S V B E A U T I F U L G T R
O Y A L E W G M P O S I T I V E B G Q M A G N I F I C E N T V M P O W E R F U L U S
A G K A W A R E F W H C A L M G A R F R E E R T D T R U E F S W E G R A T E F U L
P A S S I O N A T E R Y N D D E V O T E D O I B L E S S E D H D F A I T H F U L
L O Y A L B S M A R T B D I H A R D W O R K I N G Y E G R E A T
R E T H O U G H T F U L E C I N S P I R I N G S L A B R I L L I A N T W G W H O P E F U L
```

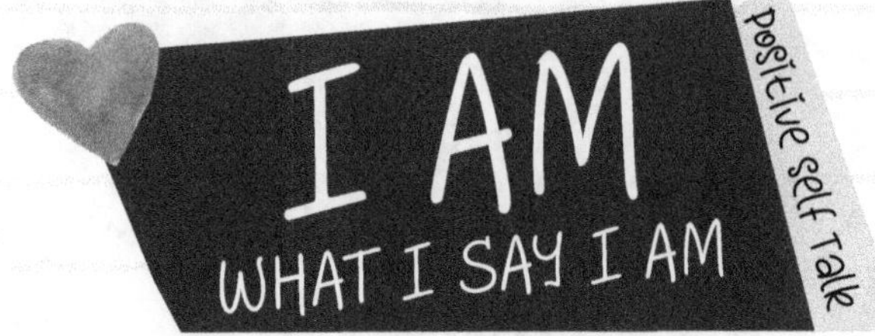

what you say to yourself creates who you are and who you will become.

mirror practice

Find a mirror and lots of energy!

Write 10 words from the "I Am" word search to practice exploring the best parts of yourself.

I am beautiful.

I am

I am

I am

I am

I am

I am

I am

I am

I am

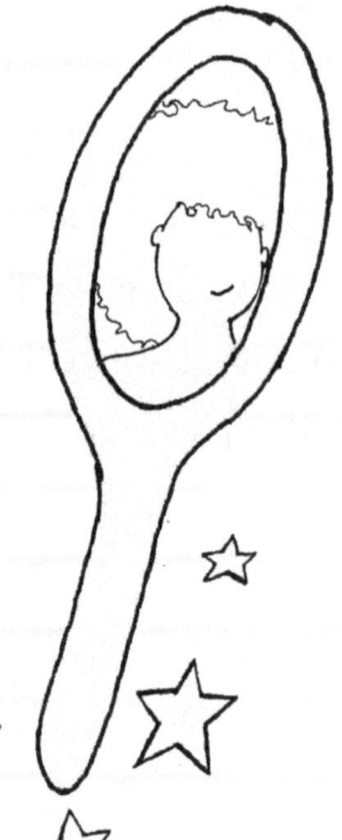

Say each ⬆ I am with confidence 3 times!

FREE SPACE: DRAW OR WRITE

How can you practice loving yourself today?

FREE SPACE: DRAW OR WRITE

List 10 ways you can respect & love your mind, body, emotions, and spirit.

FREE SPACE: DRAW OR WRITE

FREE SPACE: DRAW OR WRITE

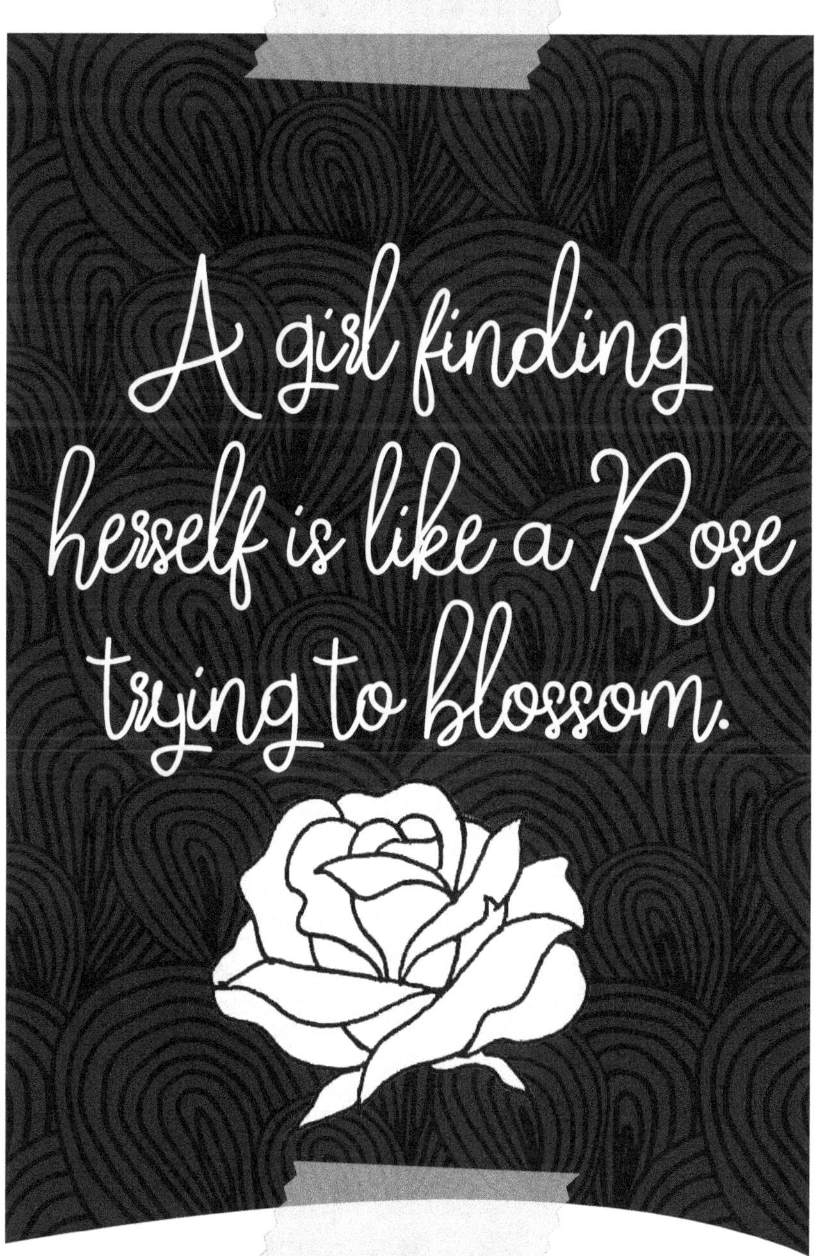
A girl finding herself is like a Rose trying to blossom.

FREE SPACE: DRAW OR WRITE

I love you...

 mirror play

It takes 30 days to start a new habit.

Read your gratitude letter aloud to yourself. Try this part of the challenge with a mirror.

... love you more.

FREE SPACE: DRAW OR WRITE

my body is beautiful

How do you take care of your body.

How do you see your body?

Draw stars where love exists in your body?

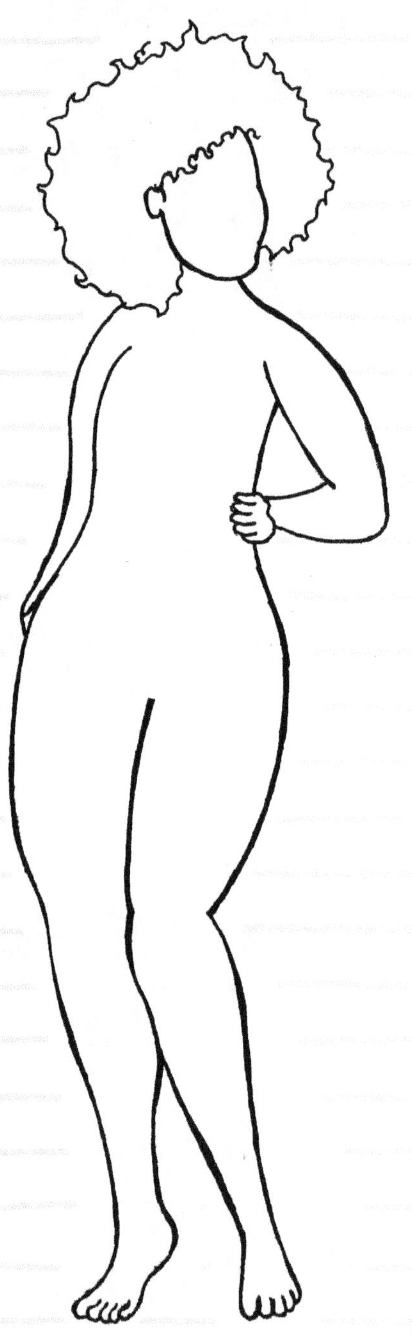

FREE SPACE: DRAW OR WRITE

FREE SPACE: DRAW OR WRITE

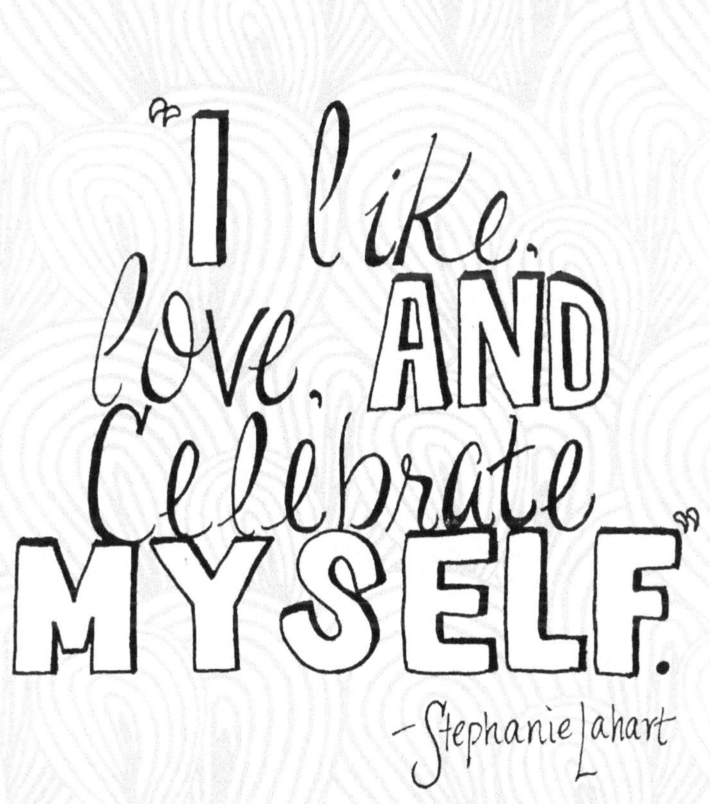

"I like,
love, AND
Celebrate
MYSELF."
-Stephanie Lahart

FREE SPACE: DRAW OR WRITE

SONG BY INELLA D. REDMOND

Cuss words, cuss words, not for me.
Cuss words, cuss words, food for snakes.
Little cuss words, food for frogs.
Big cuss words, food for snakes.
I don't cuss, I don't swear,
Don't spit cuss words in the air.

If a friend lets a cuss slip,
I don't ride that sinking ship.
I say snake food fast and quick!

Some kids say cuss words everyday
On the streets, on the bus
At school, at home, at work or play;
But I don't cuss and I don't swear
I don't spit cuss words in the air.

Cuss words, cuss words, not for me
Cuss words, cuss words, food for snakes
I don't cuss and I don't swear and
I don't spit cuss words in the air.

In what ways can words hurt your feelings?

How can you use words to encourage yourself when you feel down?

Happiness

Is happiness connected to love?

In what ways do you make yourself happy?

Draw or write what you experience when you're feeling happy?

tonight's reflection

What was it like to love yourself 1st today?

List 10 things you are grateful for.

day three
3
letter of gratitude

reflect

morning routine

Create your safe space

Close your eyes.
Inhale Deep
Exhale
(repeat 5 times)
Open your eyes.

List 5 things you are grateful for this morning.

List 5 things you love about yourself.

today, write a love letter to yourself!
make a list of reasons you're grateful for WHO YOU ARE?

Dear _________________________

(WRITE YOUR FIRST NAME)

I am grateful for

with love,

(SIGN YOUR NAME)

FREE SPACE: DRAW OR WRITE

FREE SPACE: DRAW OR WRITE

selfie practice 

Now that you've practiced loving yourself first for 3 days.

Make a list of the ways you promise to start loving yourself 1st.

Take a few selfies and print your photos.
Create a selfie collage with a
few items from your promises above.

FREE SPACE: DRAW OR WRITE

LOVIN' ME SCHEDULE

sunday	monday	tuesday	wednesday	thursday	friday	saturday

On rough days remember to breathe deeply and give yourself extra time to love yourself.

you don't plant your seed and eat the fruit the same day.
Give your ideas and habits time and nourishment to grow.

FREE SPACE: DRAW OR WRITE

FREE SPACE: DRAW OR WRITE

Love starts from within. In order to find love, you must first find yourself and love your flaws, so the love you want and deserve will find you.

FREE SPACE: DRAW OR WRITE

FREE SPACE: DRAW OR WRITE

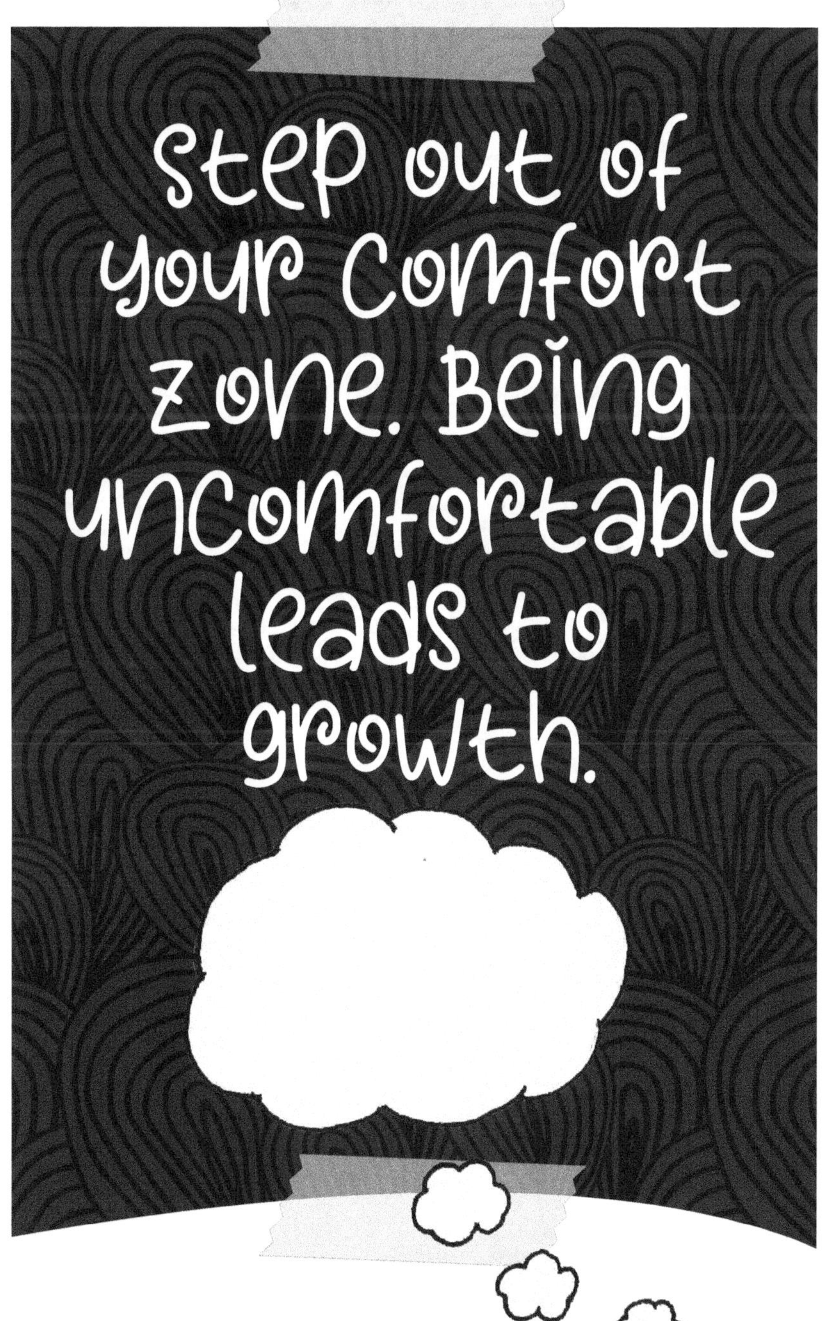
step out of your comfort zone. Being uncomfortable leads to growth.

FREE SPACE: DRAW OR WRITE

tonight's reflection

What was it like to love yourself 1st today?

List 10 things you are grateful for.

GRL
PWR

yes girl!
you did it.

glossary

detachment noun

freedom from bias or prejudice

the act of processing detaching, separation

let it go

leave anxiety behind

practice of detachment: theres no cause for worry whether things go well or ill.

grateful adjective

a feeling or showing an appreciation of kindness; thankful expressing gratitude

appreciative, glad, thankful

kindness noun

the quality of being friendly, generous, and considerate regard for the feelings, wishes, rights, or traditions of others.

affection, good will, warmth

respect noun

a feeling of deep admiration for someone or their abilities, qualities, or achievements.

regard for the feelings, wishes, rights, or traditions of others.

verb

admire (someone or something) deeply, as a result of their abilities, qualities, or achievements.

esteem, admire, honor, consideration

peace noun

freedom from disturbance; tranquility

a state or period in which there is no war or a war has ended.
calm, calmness, tranquility, silence, stillness

How does it feel to finish your first Inhale Deep Self Love Journal?

Give love RECEIVE Love
Write a letter or DM a close friend
encouraging them to share their story or
take the 3~day self love challenge.
Name your
friends

butterflyblue
PUBLISHING CO.

**FOLLOW US ON INSTAGRAM
@BUTTERFLYBLUEBOOKS**